101 Things To Do With A Potato

101 Things To Do With A Potato

BY
STEPHANIE ASHCRAFT

Gibbs Smith, Publisher
Salt Lake City

First Edition
08 07 06 05 04   20 19 18 17 16 15 14 13 12 11 10 9 8 7 6 5 4 3 2 1

Published by
Gibbs Smith, Publisher
P.O. Box 667
Layton, Utah 84041

Orders: 1.800 748.5439
www.gibbs-smith.com

Designed by Kurt Wahlner
Printed and bound in Korea

Library of Congress Cataloging-in-Publication Data

Ashcraft, Stephanie.
  101 things to do with a potato / Stephanie Ashcraft.—1st ed.
    p. cm.
  ISBN 1-58685-290-6
  1. Cookery (Potatoes) I. Title: One hundred one things to do with a potato. II. Title:
One hundred and one things to do with a potato. III. Title.
TX803.P8A84 2004
641.6'521—dc22
                          2004007810

To my father-in-law, who loves to grow delicious Idaho potatoes and who encouraged me to write a "useful" cookbook.

To my parents and mother-in-law, who give endless support, encouragement, and love.

And finally, to everyone who shared their family favorites.

CONTENTS

Baked Potatoes

Buttery Potato Fans 68 • Oriental Sour Cream Baked Potatoes 69
• Twice-Baked Garlic Potatoes 70 • Twice-Baked Ranch Potatoes 71
• Sour Cream and Cheddar Baked Potatoes 72 • Cheesy Broccoli Baked
Potatoes 73 • Chicken Salsa Baked Potatoes 74 • Pizza Baked Potatoes 75
• Creamy Ham, Peas, and Mushroom Potatoes 76

Mashed Potatoes

Traditional Mashed Potatoes and Gravy 78 • Chipotle and Pepper Jack
Mashed Potatoes 79 • Garlic Mashed Red Potatoes 80 • Heavenly Mashed
Potatoes 81 • Baked Cottage Cheese Mashed Potatoes 82 • Ranch
Mashed Potatoes 83 • Rosemary Garlic Mashed Potatoes 84 • Creamy Baked
Mashed Potatoes 85 • Mashed Sweet Potatoes 86

Fries and Wedges

Family Favorite French Fries 88 • Chili Cheese Fries 89 • Baked Oven Fries 90
• Parmesan Potato Spears 91 • Sweet Potato Fries 92 • Skillet Fried Ranch
Potatoes 93 • Cheesy Bacon Fries 94 • Italian Potato Chips 95 • Crispy Garlic
Mashed Potato Balls 96 • Baked Dijon Potato Wedges 97

Breakfast

Country Hash Browns 100 • One-Skillet Bacon Breakfast 101 • Morning
After Baked Potato Hash Browns 102 • Sour Cream Potato Pancakes 103
• Breakfast Burritos 104 • Hearty Turkey Brunch Skillet 105 • Biscuits with
Sausage Gravy 106 • Ham-and-Cheese Hash Brown Omelet 107 • Simple Bacon
Breakfast Pie 108 • Breakfast Casserole 109 • Smoked Sausage and Egg Skillet 110

Breads and Desserts

Great Grandma's Spudnuts (Idaho Donuts) 112 • Peanut Butter Chocolate
Fudge 113 • Family Favorite Potato Rolls 114 • Potato Bread 115 • Sweet Potato
Rolls 116 • Potato Chip Cookies 117 • Coconut Chocolate Bars 118
• Triple Chocolate Potato Nut Cake 119 • Ivan's Favorite Carrot Cake 120
• Sweet Potato Spice Crunch 121 • Chocolate Chip Banana Spice Bread 122
• Sweet Potato Cheesecake 123

HELPFUL HINTS

I. There are many different types of potatoes, each with different qualities that make them good for certain recipes and not for others. Here are some examples of the most common potatoes and their uses:

> **russet potatoes**—light and fluffy when baked, best used for mashed or baked potatoes, hash browns, and fries
>
> **red** or **bliss potatoes**—a waxy potato used in potato salads, roasts, and soups (other potatoes tend to get mushy)
>
> **yellow-fleshed potatoes**—a creamy-textured potato, best used in gratins
>
> **new potatoes**—small potatoes with delicate skins, great for boiling, roasting, or steaming
>
> **instant potatoes**—quick-fix mashed potatoes, best used for casseroles and meat pies

2. Buy smooth and firm potatoes with unbroken, tight skin. Avoid buying potatoes that are soft, decaying, or have excessive bruises, cuts, or cracks. Do not buy potatoes that have a green tint to them.

3. Store potatoes in a cool, dry, dark place, but do not refrigerate. The ideal temperature to store potatoes is approximately 50 degrees Fahrenheit. Keeping potatoes in a brown bag is also suggested because excessive light can cause potatoes to turn green.

5. Do not wash potatoes until you are ready to use them. Use a wire brush or pad to scrub potatoes while running them under hot water.

6. Skins can be left on or removed from potatoes, depending on personal preference, in any recipe.

7. Eye growth on potatoes is normal but occurs faster in warmer temperatures. Potatoes with vines can be used unless potatoes are soft and mushy. To use, simply break or cut off the vines.

8. Mashed Potatoes, unseasoned and not instant, can be made by scooping out the flesh of a baked potato and simply mashing it with a fork or potato masher. Traditional Mashed Potatoes can be made by using this easy recipe:

Peel and dice 5 to 6 medium russet potatoes (approximately $2^1/_4$–$2^1/_2$ pounds). Place potatoes in saucepan and cover with water. Boil 20–25 minutes, or until potatoes are tender. Drain water. Add 2 tablespoons butter and $^1/_2$ cup milk. Mash with a potato masher or mix with an electric mixer. Makes 4 cups.

9. Instant mashed potatoes are great for saving time, but are a bit saltier and not as stiff as traditional mashed potatoes. Use caution if using them as a substitute. Instant mashed potato flakes can also be used to thicken creamy soups or sauces.

10. To make baked potatoes in a slow cooker, place inside and cover and cook on low heat 8–10 hours or on high heat 4–5 hours, or until tender.

11. When boiling potatoes, just barely cover them with water. Use a pan big enough to ensure that the waterline is at least 3 to 4 inches from the top of the pan. Add a teaspoon of oil or a quick spray from a can. This will keep the potatoes from boiling over and creating a sticky mess on your stovetop.

11. Leftover peeled and cooked potatoes can be frozen in an airtight container for future use.

12. To prevent potatoes from turning brown after being peeled or cut, place the cut potatoes in a bowl of cool water or cook them immediately.

13. Small potatoes cook faster than large potatoes. Try cooking potatoes that are similar in size, or cut them in pieces, for uniform cooking.

14. For the health conscious, low fat or light ingredients can be used in all recipes.

Soups and Stews

EASY CHICKEN SOUP

I box (4.9 ounces)	**scalloped potato mix,** with seasoning packet
I can (10 ounces)	**chicken breast meat,** with liquid
4^1/$_2$ cups	**water**
^{1}/$_2$ teaspoon	**pepper**
I cup	**frozen mixed vegetables**

Mix potatoes, seasoning packet, chicken, water, and pepper together in a 2- to 3-quart saucepan. Bring to a boil, then add frozen vegetables. Simmer at a low boil 15–17 minutes, or until potatoes are tender. Makes 4–6 servings.

QUICK POTATO SOUP

2¹/₂ cups **water**
1 bag (28 ounces) **frozen O'Brien potatoes**
(cubed with peppers and onions)
2¹/₂ cups **milk**
salt and pepper, to taste
6 to 8 **slices bacon,** cooked and crumbled

Pour water into a 3- to 4-quart soup pan and bring to a boil. Stir in frozen potatoes and return to boil. Reduce to medium-low heat and simmer 10–15 minutes, or until potatoes are tender. Reduce heat to low. Stir in milk, salt, and pepper. Heat 7 minutes, or until soup is heated through. Do not boil after milk has been added. Stir in bacon right before serving. Garnish with crushed croutons. Makes 6 servings.

VARIATION: Melt ¹/₄ pound Velveeta cheese into soup after adding milk.

CHEESY VEGETABLE CHOWDER

2 cups	**water**
I teaspoon	**granulated chicken bouillon**
2 cups	**yellow-fleshed** or **red potatoes,** peeled and diced to $1/2$-inch cubes
2 cups	**frozen mixed vegetables**
$1/4$ cup	**chopped onion**
I can (15 ounces)	**cream style corm**
8 ounces	**Velveeta cheese**
$1/2$ cup	**milk**

In a 2- to 3-quart saucepan, bring water to a boil. Dissolve bouillon in boiling water. Stir in potatoes, mixed vegetables, and onion. Cover and simmer on medium-low heat 15 minutes, or until potatoes are tender. Add corn, cheese, and milk. Heat 5–7 minutes, stirring constantly until cheese is melted. Makes 6 servings.

INSTANT POTATO SOUP MIX

1 3/4 cups	**instant mashed potato flakes**
1 1/2 cups	**nonfat dry milk**
1 tablespoon	**granulated chicken bouillon**
2 tablespoons	**dried minced onion**
1 teaspoon	**parsley**
1/2 teaspoon	**thyme**
1/4 teaspoon	**pepper**

In a bowl, mix all ingredients together. Store dry soup mix in an airtight container. To make one serving, combine 1/2 cup dry soup mix with 1 cup hot water. Makes 7 servings.

CHEDDAR POTATO SOUP

4 to 5	**russet potatoes,** peeled and cubed
1 cup	**baby carrots,** cut in thirds
1 tablespoon	**dried minced onion**
3/4 teaspoon	**salt**
1/2 cup	**butter** or **margarine**
1/2 cup	**flour**
2 cups	**milk**
1 cup	**chicken broth**
2 cups	**grated cheddar cheese**
1/2 teaspoon	**pepper**

Place potatoes, carrots, onion, and salt in a large soup pan. Cover vegetables with water and bring to a boil. Simmer over medium heat 20 minutes, or until tender.

In a separate pan, melt butter, then stir in flour. Whisk in milk and chicken broth. Cook over medium heat until it begins to thicken. Pour into cooked vegetables. Stir in cheese and pepper. Garnish with grated cheddar cheese. Makes 8–10 servings.

HEARTY BROCCOLI VEGETABLE SOUP

2 tablespoons	**chicken bouillon**
8 cups	**boiling water,** divided
2	**large russet potatoes,** diced
2	**large carrots,** peeled and grated
1	**small onion,** chopped
2 cups	**chopped broccoli**
1/2 cup	**diced celery,** optional
1/2 cup	**butter** or **margarine**
3/4 cup	**flour**
1 cup	**Cheese Whiz**

In a 4-quart soup pan, dissolve bouillon in 4 cups boiling water. Add potatoes, carrots, onion, broccoli, and celery, if desired, and cook on medium heat 15–20 minutes, or until tender.

In a large frying pan, melt margarine, then slowly stir in flour. Add remaining water to vegetables and stir until soup begins to thicken. Stir Cheese Whiz into butter and flour mixture, then add cheese sauce to vegetables. Continue to cook on low heat until soup is thoroughly heated. Garnish with fresh parsley. Makes 10–12 servings.

SIMPLE POTATO SOUP

$^1/_2$	**medium onion,** chopped
2 tablespoons	**butter** or **margarine**
3 to 5	**large russet potatoes,** cubed
$6^1/_4$ cups	**water**
2 teaspoons	**salt**
1 teaspoon	**pepper**
1 can (12 ounces)	**evaporated milk**
1 can (15.25 ounces)	**whole kernel corn,** drained

In a 4-quart soup pan, saute onion and butter together until onion becomes transparent. Add potatoes, water, salt, and pepper and bring to a boil. Gently boil potatoes 15 minutes, or until tender. Reduce to low heat. Stir in milk and corn. Cook on low heat an additional 5 minutes. Garnish with grated cheddar cheese. Makes 8–10 servings.

VARIATION: Add 1 $^1/_2$ cups ham, cooked and diced.

SAUSAGE CORN CHOWDER

I tablespoon	**dried minced onion**
4 to 5	**medium russet potatoes,** peeled and cubed
I teaspoon	**Italian seasoning**
2 cups	**water**
I teaspoon	**salt**
$^1/_2$ teaspoon	**pepper**
I can (12 ounces)	**evaporated milk**
12 ounces	**sausage,** browned and drained
I can (15.25 ounces)	**whole kernel corn,** drained
I can (14.75 ounces)	**cream style corn**

In a 4-quart soup pan, bring onion, potatoes, Italian seasoning, water, salt, and pepper to a low boil. Reduce heat and simmer, uncovered, 15–20 minutes, or until potatoes are tender. Add milk, sausage, and corn. Cook over low heat, uncovered, an additional 5–7 minutes, or until heated through. Do not boil after milk has been added. Makes 8 servings.

TOMATO BEEF STEW

I to 2 pounds	**chuck beef** or **round steak,** cubed
6 to 7	**medium red potatoes,** peeled and cubed
I bag (16 ounces)	**baby carrots,** cut in thirds
I	**medium onion,** chopped
I can (28 ounces)	**crushed tomatoes,** with liquid
2 cans	**water,** measured from tomato can
I tablespoon	**rosemary**
	salt and pepper, to taste

In a 6-quart stock pot, brown beef. Add potatoes, carrots, onion, tomatoes, water, rosemary, salt, and pepper. Bring to a boil, then simmer on medium-low heat 25–30 minutes, or until potatoes and carrots are tender. Makes 8–10 servings.

VARIATION: Simmer in a 6- to 7-quart slow cooker. Meat does not need to be browned for slow cooker stew. Reduce amount of water to I 1/2 cans. Cover and cook on low heat 6–8 hours or on high heat 3–4 hours.

AUNT TAMMI'S POTATO SOUP

6 to 8 **medium russet potatoes,** diced
1 **medium onion,** chopped
1 teaspoon **salt**
2 cups **milk**
1 teaspoon **parsley**

Place potatoes, onion, and salt in a 4-quart soup pan. Cover potatoes with water and bring to a low boil. Lower heat and simmer, uncovered, 15–20 minutes, or until potatoes are tender. Add milk and parsley. Cook an additional 10 minutes over medium-low heat. Do not boil after milk has been added. Makes 8 servings.

VARIATION: Add 1 cup ham, cooked and cubed, or 1 cup carrots and celery, peeled and diced, with potatoes and onion.

SALADS

BASIC POTATO SALAD

3 **medium red potatoes**
I teaspoon **salt**
2 **eggs**
¹/₂ cup **Miracle Whip**

Bring potatoes to a boil in water with salt, then simmer over medium-low heat 20 minutes, or until tender. Drain water and allow potatoes to cool to room temperature.

In a saucepan, completely cover eggs with cold water. Bring to a boil over high heat 10–12 minutes. Drain, then run cold water over eggs until cooled. Peel hard-boiled eggs. Remove egg yolk and set aside.

Once cooled, dice potatoes and egg whites and place in a serving bowl. Stir in Miracle Whip. Crumble egg yolks over top. Refrigerate 3 or more hours before serving. Makes 2 servings.

GRANDMA ASHCRAFT'S MUSTARD POTATO SALAD

5 to 6	**large russet potatoes,** peeled and cubed*
I cup	**Miracle Whip**
1/4 cup	**evaporated milk**
I teaspoon	**vinegar**
I teaspoon	**salt**
I tablespoon	**mustard**
1/4 cup	**dried minced onions**

Boil potatoes until tender. Remove from heat and drain. Allow potatoes to cool to room temperature.

In a large bowl, mix Miracle Whip, milk, vinegar, salt, mustard, and onion together. Fold potatoes into mixture. Chill and serve. Makes 8 servings.

VARIATION: Add hard-boiled eggs, olives, pickles, or radishes.

*Approximately 2 1/2 pounds of potatoes.

HOT MASHED POTATO SALAD

4	**medium russet potatoes,** diced
¹/₄ cup	**dill pickles,** diced
¹/₄ teaspoon	**dried minced onion**
2 tablespoons	**mustard**
1 tablespoon	**mayonnaise**
1 tablespoon	**salsa**
1 tablespoon	**pickle juice,** from dill pickle jar
¹/₄ teaspoon	**salt**
	pepper, to taste

Boil diced potatoes 15 minutes, or until tender. Drain and mash potatoes with potato masher. Stir in pickles, onion, mustard, mayonnaise, salsa, pickle juice, salt, and pepper. Serve immediately. Makes 6 servings.

HOT BACON-POTATO SALAD

6 **medium yellow-fleshed** or **red potatoes,** peeled and cubed
4 to 6 **slices bacon,** cooked and crumbled
1 **small onion,** chopped
1/3 cup **cider vinegar**
1 tablespoon **sugar**
2 tablespoons **minced fresh parsley**
1 teaspoon **salt**
1/2 teaspoon **pepper**

In a 2-quart saucepan, cover potatoes with water and bring to a boil over high heat. Reduce to medium-low heat and simmer 15–20 minutes, or until tender. Drain. Crumble bacon over hot potatoes.

In a separate small saucepan, bring onion, vinegar, sugar, parsley, salt, and pepper to a boil. Stir into potato-and-bacon mixture. Serve immediately. Makes 4–5 servings.

DELUXE BAKED POTATO SALAD

5 to 6 **medium russet potatoes**
$^3/_4$ cup **sour cream**
$^3/_4$ cup **mayonnaise**
$^1/_2$ cup **chopped onion**
salt and pepper, to taste
8 **slices bacon,** cooked and crumbled
grated cheddar cheese

Preheat oven to 425 degrees.

Poke each potato twice with a fork. Bake 50–60 minutes, or until tender. Allow potatoes to cool to room temperature, then cut into $^1/_2$-inch cubes, with or without skins.

In 2-quart bowl, combine sour cream, mayonnaise, and onion, then fold in potatoes. Cover and refrigerate 3 hours. Before serving, add salt and pepper, then sprinkle crumbled bacon evenly over top. Garnish with grated cheddar cheese. Makes 6–8 servings.

BACON-RANCH POTATO SALAD

15 to 16 **medium red potatoes***
2 cups **mayonnaise**
$^1/_2$ cup **chopped green onion**
1 envelope **ranch dressing mix**
1 pound **bacon,** cooked and crumbled

Place potatoes in large pot and cover with water. Boil 20–25 minutes, or until tender. Drain, then run cold water over potatoes. Once potatoes are cooled, cut into cubes.

In a large bowl, combine mayonnaise, green onion, and ranch mix. Gently stir in potatoes. Cover and refrigerate at least 3 hours. Just before serving, stir in crumbled bacon. Makes 10–12 servings.

* Approximately 5 pounds of potatoes.

INSTANT DILL POTATO SALAD

1/4 cup	**Miracle Whip**
2 tablespoons	**apple juice**
1 tablespoon	**dried minced onion**
1 teaspoon	**dill**
1/4 teaspoon	**garlic powder**
1 can (15 ounces)	**sliced potatoes,** drained

Mix Miracle Whip, apple juice, onion, dill, and garlic powder together with a wire whisk. Stir in potato slices. Serve immediately or chill until ready to serve. Makes 2–4 servings.

CHILLED MASHED POTATO SALAD

4 to 4 1/2 cups	**mashed potatoes***
1/2 teaspoon	**salt**
1/4 teaspoon	**pepper**
1/4 cup	**sweet pickle relish**
3	**eggs**
1/3 cup	**chopped onion**
1/2 cup	**Miracle Whip**

In a saucepan, completely cover eggs with cold water. Bring to a boil over high heat 10–12 minutes. Drain, then run cold water over eggs until cooled. Peel hard-boiled eggs, then dice.

In large bowl, combine all ingredients and mix together. Chill at least 3 hours. Makes 4–6 servings.

* See page 10, Helpful Hints, for Mashed Potatoes recipe.

TANGY DIJON POTATO SALAD

7 to 8	**new potatoes,** cubed
1/4 cup	**Dijon mustard**
2 tablespoons	**cider vinegar**
2 teaspoons	**minced garlic**
1/2 teaspoon	**salt**
1/4 teaspoon	**pepper**
1/3 cup	**olive oil**

In a 2-quart saucepan, cover potatoes with water and bring to a boil over high heat. Reduce to medium-low heat and simmer 15–20 minutes, or until tender. Drain.

In a 2-quart bowl, combine mustard, vinegar, garlic, salt, and pepper. Slowly whisk in oil until well blended. Stir in potatoes. Serve hot or chilled. Makes 4–6 servings.

VARIATION: Add sliced olives, chopped green onions, or cooked and crumbled bacon.

Main Dishes

AMY'S MEAT-FILLED ROLLS

1 pound	**ground beef** or **sausage**
2 tablespoons	**dried onion**
2	**medium red** or **russet potatoes,** peeled and grated
1 can (10.5 ounces)	**cream of mushroom soup,** condensed
1/4 teaspoon	**garlic** or **celery salt**
12 to 15	**pre-made dinner rolls**
12 to 15	**slices cheddar cheese**

Cook meat, onion, and potatoes together in a large frying pan on medium-high heat 15 minutes, or until meat is thoroughly browned and potatoes are tender. Stir soup and salt into mixture and set aside.

Scoop out centers of rolls, then fill with meat mixture. Place rolls evenly over a baking sheet and top with a slice of cheddar cheese. Broil in oven 2–3 minutes, or until cheese is melted. Makes 6–8 servings.

CREAMY POT ROAST

6 to 10	**red potatoes,** cubed
$^1/_2$ to 1 pound	**baby carrots,** halved
3-pound	**beef roast**
$^1/_2$	**medium onion,** thinly sliced
1 envelope	**onion soup mix**
$^1/_2$ cup	**water**
2 cans (10.5 ounces each)	**cream of mushroom soup,** condensed

Layer half of potatoes and carrots in a greased 5- to 7-quart slow cooker. Set roast over top. Place onion and remaining carrots and potatoes over meat. Mix onion soup mix and water together, then pour over top. Spread cream soup over roast and vegetables. Cover and cook on low heat 8–10 hours. Makes 6–8 servings.

EASY CHICKEN POTPIE

1 can (12.5 ounces)	**chicken breast chunks,** drained
1 cup	**milk**
2 cans (10.75 ounces each)	**cream of chicken soup,** condensed
1 bag (16 ounces)	**frozen mixed vegetables**
$^1/_2$ teaspoon	**salt**
2 cans (14.5 ounces each)	**diced new potatoes,** drained
2 cans (8 ounces each)	**crescent rolls**

Preheat oven to 400 degrees.

In a large frying pan, combine chicken, milk, and soup. Cook over medium-low heat, stirring constantly. When it starts bubbling, add mixed vegetables, salt, and potatoes. Simmer on low heat 5–7 minutes.

Roll out one can of crescent roll dough and place in bottom of a 9 x 13-inch pan. Pour filling over crust. Separate second can of crescent rolls. Place triangles over top, covering as much as possible. Bake 15 minutes, or until crescents are golden brown. Makes 8 servings.

HONEY MUSTARD CHICKEN AND HASH BROWN CASSEROLE

2 cans (10.75 ounces each)	**cream of chicken soup,** condensed
3/4 cup	**mayonnaise**
1/2 cup	**milk**
1/4 cup	**honey**
2 tablespoons	**mustard**
2 to 3 cups	**chicken,** cooked and cubed*
1 bag (30 ounces)	**frozen shredded hash browns**

Preheat oven to 350 degrees.

In a large bowl, mix soup, mayonnaise, milk, honey, and mustard together until smooth. Stir in chicken and hash browns. Spread in a greased 9 x 13-inch pan. Cover with aluminum foil and bake 40–50 minutes. Uncover and bake an additional 10–15 minutes, or until golden brown and bubbly around edges. Makes 8 servings.

* Canned chicken breast may be substituted.

CREAMY CASSEROLE

1 bag (26 ounces)	**frozen shredded hash browns**
1 pound	**ground beef,** browned and drained
1/2 cup	**chopped onion**
1 1/2 cups	**frozen peas**
2 cups	**half-and-half** or **milk**
2 cans (10.75 ounces each)	**cream of chicken soup,** condensed
1 cup	**grated cheddar cheese**

Preheat oven to 350 degrees.

Place hash browns on bottom of a greased 9 x 13-inch pan. Spread beef and onion over hash browns. Arrange peas over top and set aside.

In a mixing bowl, combine half-and-half and soup. Pour over casserole. Sprinkle cheese over top and bake 60–70 minutes, or until golden brown and bubbly around edges. Makes 8 servings.

BEEF AND SCALLOPED POTATOES

5 to 6 **large russet potatoes,** sliced*
1 cup **chopped onion,** divided
2 teaspoons **salt,** divided
1 cup **grated Swiss** or **cheddar cheese**
1 1/2 pounds **ground beef**
3/4 cup **sour cream**
1/2 cup **crushed saltine crackers**

Preheat oven to 350 degrees.

Layer potatoes, 3/4 cup onion, 1 teaspoon salt, and cheese evenly in a greased 9 x 13-inch pan.

In a separate bowl, mix beef, sour cream, saltines, remaining onion, and 1 teaspoon salt. Place beef mixture over potato mixture. Bake covered with aluminum foil 30 minutes. Remove foil and bake an additional 20 minutes, or until meat and potatoes are done. Makes 8 servings.

*Approximately 2 1/2 pounds of potatoes.

SMOTHERED CUBE STEAKS

4	**cube steaks***
	salt and pepper, to taste
4 to 5	**yellow-fleshed potatoes**
1	**medium sweet onion,** thinly sliced
2 cans (10.5 ounces each)	**cream of mushroom soup,** condensed

Preheat oven to 350 degrees.

Place cube steaks in bottom of a lightly greased 9 x 13-inch pan. Add salt and pepper to meat. Peel and thinly slice potatoes. Layer potatoes, then onion, over steaks. Spread soup over top. Cover with aluminum foil. Bake 70–75 minutes, or until meat is done. Makes 4–6 servings.

* Approximately 1 pound total weight.

CREAMY BROCCOLI POTATO BAKE

1 can (10.5 ounces)	**cream of broccoli soup,** condensed
3/4 cup	**milk**
1/2 teaspoon	**salt**
1/4 teaspoon	**pepper**
1 1/2 cups	**cubed ham**
2 cups	**frozen chopped broccoli**
1 bag (24 ounces)	**frozen shredded hash browns**
1 cup	**crushed cornflakes**

Preheat oven to 350 degrees.

In a large bowl, stir together soup, milk, salt, pepper, ham, and broccoli. Fold in hash browns. Spread mixture evenly over the bottom of a lightly greased 9 x 13-inch pan. Sprinkle cornflakes over top. Cover with aluminum foil. Bake 45–55 minutes, or until hot in the center and bubbly around edges. For a crispier top, remove aluminum foil last 10–15 minutes of baking. Makes 8 servings.

AUNT COSETTE'S GNOCCHI POTATO DUMPLINGS

16 cups	**water**
2 teaspoons	**salt**
2	**medium russet potatoes,** baked, peeled, and mashed*
2 cups	**flour**
2 jars (26 ounces each)	**chunky spaghetti sauce,** hot

In a 6-quart soup pan, bring water and salt to a boil.

In a separate bowl, combine warm mashed potatoes and flour to make a uniform and tender dough (not sticky). Divide dough into four sections. Roll each section into a $3/4$-inch-thick rope, then cut into $3/4$-inch pieces. Roll pieces into balls. Push your thumb into the center of the ball, making a dent. Drop into boiling water. Balls will fall to bottom of pan. Once balls float back to the top, remove and strain 2–3 minutes. Repeat until all the dough is cooked. Transfer dumplings to a serving dish and cover with spaghetti sauce. Serve immediately. Makes 6–8 servings.

* Approximately 1 pound total weight.

TATER TOT CASSEROLE

I pound **ground beef** or **turkey**
$^1/_2$ cup **chopped onion**
I can (14.5 ounces) **French style green beans,** liquid reserved
I can (10.5 ounces) **cream of mushroom soup,** condensed
I bag (16 ounces) **tater tots**

Preheat oven to 350 degrees.

Brown meat with onion. Drain and spread in a lightly greased 8 x 8-inch or 9 x 9-inch pan. Drain green beans, reserving liquid in a separate bowl. Layer green beans evenly over meat. Mix reserved liquid with soup and spread over top. Place tater tots lengthwise over soup and cover entire surface. Bake 25–30 minutes, or until tater tots are brown and crispy. Makes 4–6 servings.

POTATO CRUST PIZZA

12 to 16 ounces **ground sausage***
1 **small onion,** chopped
2¹/₂ to 3 cups **russet potatoes,** peeled and thinly sliced
1 jar (26 ounces) **chunky vegetable spaghetti sauce**
2 cups **grated mozzarella cheese**
grated Parmesan cheese, for garnish

Preheat oven to 350 degrees.

Brown sausage and onion together.

Spread potatoes in bottom of a greased 9 x 13-inch pan. Spread sausage and onion over top. Cover evenly with spaghetti sauce. Cover with aluminum foil and bake 30–35 minutes. Remove from oven and sprinkle cheese over top. Return uncovered to oven for an additional 10–15 minutes, or until cheese is melted and sauce is bubbly. Garnish with grated Parmesan cheese. Makes 6–8 servings.

VARIATION: Add pepperoni, olive, or mushroom slices before spaghetti sauce.

* Ground beef or turkey may be substituted.

MASHED POTATO PIZZA

4 servings	**instant mashed potato flakes**
I can (10 ounces)	**pizza crust dough***
2 cups	**grated cheddar cheese,** divided
I jar (3 ounces)	**real bacon bits,** divided
1/4 cup	**green onions,** chopped

Prepare instant mashed potatoes according to package directions.

Preheat oven to 400 degrees.

Press pizza dough into a lightly greased 9 x 13-inch pan. Bake 8 minutes.

Stir half of cheese and half of bacon bits into warm mashed potatoes.
Spread potatoes over partially baked crust. Sprinkle green onions,
remaining bacon bits, and remaining cheese over potato layer. Bake
an additional 10–12 minutes, or until cheese is completely melted.
Garnish with sour cream. Makes 6–8 servings.

* If using a pizza crust that covers a baking sheet, prepare 6 servings
of instant mashed potatoes instead of 4.

SAUCY MEAT AND POTATOES

5 to 6 **medium red potatoes,** peeled and thinly sliced
$3/4$ cup **steak sauce,** divided
2 pounds **ground beef**
$3/4$ cup **seasoned bread crumbs**
$2/3$ cup **chopped onion**

Preheat oven to 350 degrees.

Lay potato slices on bottom of a greased 8 x 8-inch or 9 x 9-inch pan.

In a large bowl, combine $1/4$ cup steak sauce, beef, bread crumbs, and onion. Press mixture evenly over potato layer. Spread remaining steak sauce over the top. Bake uncovered 65–75 minutes, or until beef is completely cooked through. Makes 4–6 servings.

COUNTRY SKILLET STEAK AND POTATOES

4	**T-bone steaks***
$1/4$ cup	**dried onion**
1 tablespoon	**flour**
1 can (10.5 ounces)	**cream of mushroom soup,** condensed
1 can (4 ounces)	**sliced mushrooms,** drained
3	**large russet potatoes,** diced
1 teaspoon	**salt**
$1/4$ teaspoon	**pepper**

In an electric skillet with lid, brown meat and set aside.

In a bowl, combine remaining ingredients, then pour over steaks in skillet. Cover and simmer at 250 degrees for 50 minutes, or until steaks are done and potatoes are tender. Turn meat and potatoes every 15–20 minutes for even cooking. Makes 4–6 servings.

* Sirloin or cubed steak may be substituted, but cooking time will vary depending on the thickness of the meat.

MASHED POTATO TACO PIE

I pound	**ground beef,** browned and drained
I envelope	**taco seasoning**
I can (8 ounces)	**tomato sauce**
I can (15.25 ounces)	**whole kernel corn,** drained
I can (14.75 ounces)	**cream style corn**
4 cups	**mashed potatoes***

Preheat oven to 350 degrees.

In a bowl, combine beef, taco seasoning, and tomato sauce. Layer beef mixture, corn, and potatoes in a greased 8 x 8-inch or 9 x 9-inch pan. Bake uncovered 20–25 minutes, or until hot in the center and bubbly around edges. Makes 4 servings.

* See page 10, Helpful Hints, for Mashed Potatoes recipe.

CREAMY MUSHROOM SHEPHERD'S PIE

I pound **ground beef**
$^1/_4$ cup **chopped onion**
I can (4 ounces) **mushroom pieces,** drained
I can (14.5 ounces) **green beans,** drained
I can (10.5 ounces) **cream of mushroom soup,** condensed
4 cups **mashed potatoes***

Preheat oven to 350 degrees.

Brown beef with onion and drain. Stir in mushrooms, green beans, and soup. Spread mixture in a greased 8 x 8-inch or 9 x 9-inch pan. Spoon potatoes evenly over top. Bake uncovered 20–25 minutes, or until hot in the center and bubbly around edges. Makes 4 servings.

* See page 10, Helpful Hints, for Mashed Potatoes recipe.

STUFFED SEASONED MEAT LOAF ROLL

1 pound	**ground beef**
1/2 cup	**quick oats**
1	**egg,** beaten
1/2 cup	**milk**
1/2 teaspoon	**salt**
1/4 teaspoon	**pepper**
1/4 cup	**dried minced onion**
1/3 cup	**bread crumbs**
2 cups	**mashed potatoes,** seasoned with garlic salt*
1 cup	**grated Monterey Jack** or **cheddar cheese**
1 cup	**ketchup**

Preheat oven to 350 degrees.

Combine beef, oats, egg, milk, salt, pepper, and onion in a large bowl and set aside.

Spread bread crumbs over long piece of waxed paper. Lay beef mixture over bread crumbs about 1/2 inch thick in the shape of a rectangle. Spread potatoes over top, leaving about 1/2 inch around the edges. Sprinkle cheese over potatoes. Use waxed paper to roll meat in jelly-roll fashion, with potatoes in the middle. Pinch the ends closed and place meat roll in a lightly greased bread pan. Pour ketchup over top. Bake 50–60 minutes, or until meat is done in the middle. Makes 6 servings.

* See page 10, Helpful Hints, for Mashed Potatoes recipe.

ROASTED CHICKEN AND VEGETABLES

6 to 8 **red potatoes,** cubed
I pound **baby carrots,** cut in thirds
3 to 4 **boneless, skinless chicken breasts**
I **medium onion,** thinly sliced
I envelope **onion soup mix**
$^1/_4$ cup **water**

Preheat oven to 350 degrees.

Layer potatoes and carrots in bottom of a greased 9 x 13-inch pan. Place chicken over vegetables, then arrange onion over chicken.

Mix soup mix and water together, then drizzle over chicken and veggies. Cover with aluminum foil. Bake 60–65 minutes, or until chicken is done and vegetables are tender. Makes 4–6 servings.

BEN'S JAPANESE CURRY

4 cups **water**
2 **medium russet potatoes,** peeled and cubed
1 **medium onion,** chopped
12 **baby carrots,** thinly sliced
2 **boneless, skinless chicken breasts,** cubed
1 packet (4.4 ounces) **Vermont House Apples and Honey Curry,** cubed*

Bring water to a boil in a medium saucepan. Stir in potatoes, onion, and carrots. Cover and boil 5 minutes. Add chicken. Cover and boil an additional 5–7 minutes, or until chicken is done and vegetables are tender. Reduce heat and add curry cubes. Stir until curry is dissolved. If thinner curry is desired, add water by the tablespoon until desired consistency is reached. Makes 6–8 servings.

VARIATION: For stronger flavor and larger portions, use two packets of curry, increase water to 5 cups and add more potatoes and carrots.

* Vermont House Apples and Honey Curry can be found in Oriental or Japanese stores. Golden House Curry may be substituted and is available in the Oriental section of most major grocery stores.

SIDE DISHES

AU GRATIN HASH BROWNS

1 bag (24–26 ounces)	**frozen O'Brien potatoes,** thawed*
1/3 cup	**butter** or **margarine**
2 cups	**half-and-half**
1 teaspoon	**salt**
1/2 teaspoon	**pepper**
1 cup	**grated cheddar cheese**

Preheat oven to 350 degrees.

Place hash browns in a lightly greased 9 x 13-inch pan and set aside.

In a saucepan, warm butter and half-and-half over medium-low heat until butter is completely melted. Stir in salt and pepper. Pour over hash browns. Sprinkle cheese over top. Cover with aluminum foil. Bake 60–70 minutes, or until golden brown around the edges. Makes 8–10 servings.

* O'Brien potatoes are cubed, with peppers and onion.

CHEESY POTATOES

³/₄ cup	**Cheez Whiz**
1 cup	**sour cream**
1 can (10.5 ounces)	**cream of mushroom soup,** condensed
¹/₂ cup	**butter** or **margarine,** melted and divided
1 package (30 ounces)	**frozen shredded hash browns,** thawed
¹/₂ cup	**seasoned bread crumbs**

Preheat oven to 350 degrees.

Stir Cheez Whiz, sour cream, soup, ¹/₃ cup melted butter, and hash browns together in a large bowl. Spread potato mixture evenly in a greased 9 x 13-inch pan.

In a separate bowl, mix bread crumbs and remaining butter together and sprinkle over top. Bake uncovered 45–50 minutes, or until bubbly around edges. Makes 8–10 servings.

CHIVE 'N' POTATO CASSEROLE

4 cups	**mashed potatoes***
I cup	**sour cream**
I package (8 ounces)	**cream cheese,** softened
I tablespoon	**chives**
$1/2$ teaspoon	**garlic powder**
$1/3$ cup	**bread crumbs**
I tablespoon	**butter** or **margarine,** melted

Preheat oven to 350 degrees.

In a large bowl, combine potatoes, sour cream, cream cheese, chives, and garlic powder. Spread into a greased 2-quart casserole dish. Sprinkle bread crumbs over potatoes, then drizzle butter over top. Bake 50 minutes. Makes 6–8 servings.

* See page 10, Helpful Hints, for Mashed Potatoes recipe.

CORN BREAD STUFFING POTATOES

I bag (24 ounces)	**frozen hash browns**
2 cups	**sour cream**
$^1/_2$ cup	**butter** or **margarine,** melted
$^1/_4$ cup	**dry minced onion***
I can (10.75 ounces)	**cream of chicken soup,** condensed
I cup	**grated cheddar cheese**
I bag (6 ounces)	**seasoned corn bread stuffing mix**

Preheat oven to 350 degrees.

In a large bowl, mix all ingredients except stuffing mix. Spread into a greased 9 x 13-inch pan. Sprinkle stuffing mix over top. Bake 35–40 minutes, or until heated through and bubbly around edges. Makes 8–10 servings.

* $^1/_2$ cup chopped onion may be substituted.

EASY BAKED HASH BROWNS

2 cans (10.75 ounces each) **cream of potato soup,** condensed*
1 1/2 cups **grated cheddar cheese**
1 1/2 cups **cubed fully cooked ham**
1 bag (26–32 ounces) **frozen shredded hash browns,** thawed
1 cup **french fried onions**

Preheat oven to 350 degrees.

In a large bowl, combine soup, cheese, ham, and hash browns together. Press into a greased 9 x 13-inch pan. Bake uncovered 55–65 minutes, or until golden brown and bubbly around edges. During last 5–10 minutes of cooking time, sprinkle french fried onions over top. Makes 8–10 servings.

* Cream of mushroom or chicken soups may be substituted.

POTLUCK POTATOES

1 bag (24 ounces)	**frozen shredded hash browns**
2 cups	**sour cream**
$^1/_2$ cup	**butter** or **margarine,** melted
$^1/_2$ cup	**chopped onion**
2 cans (10.75 ounces each)	**cream of chicken soup,** condensed
1 $^1/_2$ cups	**grated cheddar cheese**
1 $^1/_2$ cups	**crushed cornflakes**

Preheat oven to 350 degrees.

In a large microwave-safe bowl, microwave frozen hash browns 4 minutes on high. Stir sour cream, butter, onion, soup, and cheese into potatoes. Spread mixture evenly into a greased 9 x 13-inch pan. Sprinkle cornflakes over top. Bake, uncovered, 45–50 minutes, or until bubbly around edges. Makes 8–10 servings.

OVEN-ROASTED ROSEMARY POTATOES

I bag (1.5 pounds) **small red** or **pearl potatoes**
2 tablespoons **vegetable** or **olive oil**
1 1/2 teaspoons **minced garlic**
2 tablespoons **rosemary**
I teaspoon **salt**

Preheat oven to 400 degrees.

Place potatoes and oil in a large zipper-lock plastic bag. In a small bowl, combine garlic, rosemary, and salt. Sprinkle over potatoes in bag. Close bag and shake until all the potatoes are evenly covered, then spread in a roasting pan. Cover with aluminum foil. Bake 15 minutes. Remove from oven and turn potatoes over. Bake an additional 10–15 minutes, or until done. Makes 6–8 servings.

PARSLEY POTATOES

I tablespoon	**vegetable** or **olive oil**
I	**medium onion,** chopped
I teaspoon	**minced garlic**
I can (14 ounces)	**chicken broth**
I cup	**chopped fresh parsley,** divided
I bag (1.5 pounds)	**small red potatoes**
1/2 teaspoon	**pepper**

Heat oil in a large frying pan over medium-high heat. Add onion and garlic and cook over medium heat 6–8 minutes, or until onion is translucent. Stir broth and $^3/_4$ cup parsley into onion and garlic. Bring to a boil over medium-high heat. In the frying pan, lay potatoes in a single layer. Return to boil. Reduce to medium-low heat. Cover and cook 20–25 minutes, or until potatoes are tender. Remove potatoes with slotted spoon to serving bowl. Stir pepper into sauce and pour over potatoes. Sprinkle remaining parsley over top and serve immediately. Makes 6–8 servings.

CREAMY SOUR CREAM AND CHEDDAR POTATOES

I bag (24 ounces)	**frozen O'Brien potatoes** (cubed with peppers and onions)
I ¹/₂ cups	**sour cream**
I can (10.75 ounces)	**cream of potato soup,** condensed
I ¹/₂ cups	**grated cheddar cheese**
¹/₃ cup	**green onion,** sliced
I cup	**french fried onions**

Preheat oven to 350 degrees.

In a large bowl, mix potatoes, sour cream, soup, cheese, and green onion together. Spread mixture into a greased 9 x 13-inch pan. Bake uncovered 40–50 minutes. Sprinkle french fried onions over top and bake an additional 15 minutes, or until bubbly around edges. Makes 8–10 servings.

SWISS SCALLOPED POTATOES

5 to 6 **medium red potatoes,** peeled and thinly sliced
$^1/_2$ cup **green onion,** sliced
1 $^1/_4$ cups **whipping cream** or **half-and-half**
1 teaspoon **salt**
2 tablespoons **butter** or **margarine**
1 cup **grated Swiss cheese**

Preheat oven to 350 degrees. Lay potatoes in a greased 8 x 8-inch pan. Sprinkle green onion over potatoes. Mix cream and salt together, then pour over potatoes. Place small pieces of butter evenly over top. Cover with aluminum foil. Bake 55–65 minutes, or until potatoes are tender. Sprinkle cheese over top. Return pan to oven 2–4 minutes, or until cheese melts. Makes 6 servings.

AUNT TAMMI'S SCALLOPED POTATOES

5	**large russet potatoes,** thinly sliced
I teaspoon	**salt**
$^1/_4$ cup	**butter** or **margarine,** melted
I teaspoon	**onion powder**
$^1/_4$ cup	**flour**
2$^1/_2$ cups	**milk**
I $^1/_2$ cups	**grated Monterey Jack** or **cheddar cheese**

Preheat oven to 350 degrees.

Layer potatoes in a greased 9 x 13-inch pan. Sprinkle salt over potatoes.

In a bowl, mix butter and onion powder. Whisk in flour and milk. Pour over potatoes and stir. Bake 60 minutes. Remove pan from oven and sprinkle cheese on top. Bake an additional 5–10 minutes, or until potatoes are tender and cheese is melted. Makes 8–10 servings.

LAVON'S CURRY POTATOES

$1/4$ **medium onion,** diced
1 tablespoon **butter**
2 teaspoons **curry powder**
1 **tomato,** diced
2 teaspoons **salt**
9 to 10 **medium russet potatoes,**
peeled and quartered
$1^2/3$ cups **water**

In a large soup pan, saute onion in butter. Stir in curry powder and tomato. Cook over medium-low heat until tomato skin falls off and curls up. Mash tomato with a fork. Add salt, potatoes, and water. Cover and boil approximately 20 minutes, or until water is gone and potatoes are tender. Makes 8 servings.

VARIATION: Add 2 cups chicken, cooked and cubed.

BAKED POTATOES

BUTTERY POTATO FANS

    4 **medium russet potatoes**
2 tablespoons **butter** or **margarine,** melted
2 tablespoons **vegetable** or **olive oil**
    I teaspoon **seasoned salt**
    $1/2$ cup **sour cream**

Preheat oven to 450 degrees. Lightly grease a baking sheet.

Cut unpeeled potatoes into $1/4$-inch slices, but do not cut all the way
through. Place potatoes on prepared baking sheet cut-side up. Spread
slices apart without breaking.

In small bowl, mix butter and oil together, then lightly brush mixture
over potato skins and between slices. Sprinkle with salt. Bake 40–45
minutes, or until potatoes are tender and edges are brown. Dollop each
potato with sour cream. Makes 4 servings.

ORIENTAL SOUR CREAM BAKED POTATOES

4 to 6 **medium russet potatoes**
I cup **sour cream**
I tablespoon **soy sauce**
I tablespoon **chopped chives**

Poke potatoes with fork 3 to 4 times. Bake at 400 degrees 55–60 minutes, or until potatoes are tender.*

In a bowl, mix sour cream, soy sauce, and chives together. Place a large dollop of sour cream mixture over opened baked potatoes. Makes 4–6 servings.

* See page 10, Helpful Hints, for making baked potatoes in a slow cooker.

TWICE-BAKED GARLIC POTATOES

6 to 8	**large russet potatoes**
1 cup	**milk**
1/4 cup	**butter** or **margarine**
1 1/2 teaspoons	**garlic powder**
1/2 teaspoon	**parsley**

Preheat oven to 400 degrees.

Poke potatoes with a fork twice and place on a baking sheet. Bake 50–55 minutes, or until tender. Once potatoes have cooled slightly, slice lengthwise and carefully scoop out the flesh, leaving about a 1/4-inch-thick shell.

Put the scooped-out potato into a mixing bowl and mash thoroughly. Add milk, butter, garlic powder, and parsley. Mix with an electric mixer until creamy. Spoon potato mixture back into potato shells. Bake at 350 degrees an additional 15 minutes, or until heated. Makes 6–8 servings.

VARIATION: For Cheddar and Bacon Twice-Baked Potatoes, replace garlic powder and parsley with 2 cups grated cheddar cheese and add 10 to 12 slices bacon, cooked and crumbled.

TWICE-BAKED RANCH POTATOES

4	**large russet potatoes**
I package (10 ounces)	**frozen chopped broccoli,** thawed and drained
¹/₂ cup	**ranch salad dressing**
I	**small onion,** chopped
I tablespoon	**butter** or **margarine**
I ¹/₂ teaspoons	**dried parsley**
	salt and pepper, to taste

Preheat oven to 400 degrees.

Poke potatoes with a fork twice and place on a baking sheet. Bake 50–55 minutes, or until tender. Once potatoes have cooled slightly, slice lengthwise and carefully scoop out the flesh, leaving about a ¹/₄-inch-thick shell.

Put the scooped-out potato into a mixing bowl and mash thoroughly, then add broccoli and dressing.

Saute onion and butter in a frying pan over medium heat, then add to potato mixture and mix well. Spoon mixture back into potato shells. Bake at 350 degrees an additional 15 minutes, or until heated. Sprinkle with parsley and salt and pepper. Makes 4 servings.

SOUR CREAM AND CHEDDAR BAKED POTATOES

6 to 8	**medium russet potatoes**
1/2 cup	**vegetable oil**
2 cups	**sour cream**
	salt, to taste
1/2 cup	**butter** or **margarine,** softened
1 cup	**grated cheddar cheese**
1 tablespoon	**chopped chives** or **green onion**

Preheat oven to 400 degrees.

Poke potatoes with fork 3 to 4 times. Rub a small amount of vegetable oil over potato skins. Lay potatoes on a large baking sheet. Lightly sprinkle salt over potatoes. Bake 55–60 minutes, or until potatoes are tender.

Mix sour cream, butter, and cheese together until smooth. Fold in chives or green onion. Spoon over hot baked potatoes. Makes 6–8 servings.

CHEESY BROCCOLI BAKED POTATOES

                        4 to 6 **medium russet potatoes**
        I can (10.75 ounces) **broccoli cheese soup,** condensed
                       ¹/₂ can **milk,** using soup can
                        I cup **frozen chopped broccoli**
                               sour cream
                               salt and pepper, to taste

Preheat oven to 400 degrees.

Poke potatoes with fork 3 to 4 times. Bake 55–60 minutes, or until potatoes are tender.*

In saucepan, cook soup, milk, and broccoli together until thoroughly heated. Pour over opened hot baked potatoes and top with sour cream. Makes 4–6 servings.

* See page 10, Helpful Hints, for making baked potatoes in a slow cooker.

CHICKEN SALSA BAKED POTATOES

6 to 8	**medium russet potatoes**
I can (12.5 ounces)	**chicken breast meat,** drained
I jar (16 ounces)	**chunky salsa**
I can (16 ounces)	**refried beans**
I envelope	**taco seasoning**
2 cups	**grated cheddar cheese**

Preheat oven to 400 degrees.

Poke potatoes with fork 3 to 4 times. Bake 55–60 minutes, or until potatoes are tender.*

In a 2-quart saucepan, combine chicken, salsa, beans, and taco seasoning. Cook over medium heat, stirring constantly until completely heated. Divide over opened hot baked potatoes. Sprinkle cheese over top. Garnish with sour cream and sliced olives. Makes 6–8 servings.

* See page 10, Helpful Hints, for making baked potatoes in a slow cooker.

PIZZA BAKED POTATOES

4 to 6 **medium russet potatoes**
1 1/2 cups **chunky spaghetti sauce**
1 1/4 cups **grated mozzarella cheese**

Preheat oven to 400 degrees.

Poke potatoes with fork 3 to 4 times. Bake 55–60 minutes, or until potatoes are tender.*

In saucepan, heat spaghetti sauce. Spoon sauce over opened hot baked potatoes. Sprinkle grated cheese over top. Garnish with favorite pizza toppings or sliced green onion. Makes 4–6 servings.

* See page 10, Helpful Hints, for making baked potatoes in a slow cooker.

CREAMY HAM, PEAS, AND MUSHROOM POTATOES

6 to 8	**medium russet potatoes**
¹/₃ cup	**butter** or **margarine**
¹/₂ cup	**chopped onion**
4 tablespoons	**flour**
¹/₈ teaspoon	**pepper**
3¹/₂ cups	**milk**
I package (8 ounces)	**cream cheese**
I bag (10 ounces)	**frozen peas**
2 cups	**diced cooked ham**
I can (7 ounces)	**mushroom pieces,** drained
¹/₂ teaspoon	**Worcestershire sauce**

Preheat oven to 400 degrees.

Poke potatoes with fork 3 to 4 times. Bake 55–60 minutes, or until potatoes are tender.*

In a 2-quart saucepan, saute butter and onion together until onion becomes transparent. Over low heat, stir in flour to thicken. Add remaining ingredients and stir constantly until hot, but not boiling. Serve sauce over baked potatoes. Makes 6–8 servings.

Leftover sauce can be served over basic mashed potatoes as well.

* See page 10, Helpful Hints, for making baked potatoes in a slow cooker.

MASHED POTATOES

TRADITIONAL MASHED POTATOES AND GRAVY

10 to 12	**medium russet potatoes,** peeled and diced
¹/₂ cup	**butter** or **margarine**
1 cup	**half-and-half** or **milk**
1 teaspoon	**salt**
¹/₂ teaspoon	**pepper**
2 jars (12 ounces each)	**chicken** or **beef gravy**

In a large soup pan, cover potatoes with water. Boil 20–25 minutes, or until potatoes are tender. Drain water, then add butter, half-and-half, salt, and pepper. Mash with a potato masher or mix with an electric mixer.

In a separate saucepan, warm gravy over low heat. Serve potatoes with gravy immediately. Makes 10–12 servings.

VARIATION: Add ³/₄ cup fresh chopped parsley or chives.

CHIPOTLE AND PEPPER JACK MASHED POTATOES

2½ pounds	**yellow-fleshed potatoes with skins,** cubed
2 teaspoons	**salt**
1 cup	**milk**
2 tablespoons	**butter**
1 envelope	**taco seasoning,** or to taste
1 cup	**grated pepper jack cheese**
2 tablespoons	**sour cream**
1 can (7 ounces)	**chipotle chilies in adobo,** drained and minced, with sauce reserved*
1 teaspoon	**adobo sauce,** from can

In a large saucepan, cover potatoes with cold water, then add salt. Bring to a boil. Reduce heat and boil 30 minutes.

In a small saucepan, combine milk, butter, and taco seasoning. Bring to a boil and set aside.

Drain potatoes, then return to saucepan. Stir over medium heat to dry out. Remove from heat and stir in cheese. Add milk mixture, sour cream, chipotle chilies, and 1 teaspoon of reserved adobo sauce. Mash with a potato masher or mix with an electric mixer and serve. Makes 4–6 servings.

* Chipotle chilies in adobo can be found in the Mexican section at most grocery stores.

GARLIC MASHED
RED POTATOES

5 to 6	**medium red potatoes,** cut into chunks
1/2 cup	**butter** or **margarine**
1/2 cup	**grated Romano cheese**
2 tablespoons	**minced garlic**
I teaspoon	**oregano**
I teaspoon	**salt**

In a 4-quart pan, cover potatoes with water. Bring to a boil, then simmer 20–25 minutes, or until potatoes are tender. Drain. Stir in butter, cheese, garlic, oregano, and salt. Mash with a potato masher or mix with an electric mixer. Serve immediately. Makes 4 servings.

If potatoes are too stiff, add 1/4 cup milk or half-and-half.

HEAVENLY MASHED POTATOES

5 to 6 **medium russet potatoes,** peeled and cubed
4 ounces **cream cheese,** softened
1 cup **sour cream**
$^1/_4$ cup **milk**
salt and pepper, to taste

In a 4-quart saucepan, boil potatoes 20–25 minutes, or until tender. Drain and mash with a potato masher or mix with an electric mixer. Mix in cream cheese, sour cream, and milk. Add salt and pepper. Serve immediately. Makes 4–6 servings.

BAKED COTTAGE CHEESE MASHED POTATOES

6 servings **instant mashed potatoes**
1 cup **cottage cheese**
1 cup **grated cheddar cheese**
¹/₄ cup **chopped chives**

Preheat oven to 350 degrees.

Prepare instant mashed potatoes according to package directions. Stir in cottage cheese, cheddar cheese, and chives. Spread potatoes in an 8 x 8-inch pan and bake 30–35 minutes. Makes 4 servings.

RANCH MASHED POTATOES

5 pounds	**red** or **yellow-fleshed potatoes,** peeled and cubed
2 teaspoons	**salt**
1/3 cup	**half-and-half** or **milk***
I package (8 ounces)	**cream cheese,** softened
I envelope	**ranch dressing mix**

Place potatoes in bottom of a large soup pan. Cover potatoes with water and add salt. Bring to a boil. Reduce to medium-low heat. Cook 20–25 minutes, or until tender. Drain and add half-and-half to potatoes. Mash with a potato masher or mix with an electric mixer. Mix in cream cheese and ranch dressing mix until smooth. Serve immediately. Makes 10–12 servings.

* More half-and-half or milk may be added for creamier potatoes.

ROSEMARY GARLIC MASHED POTATOES

6	**medium russet potatoes,** peeled and cubed
1/3 to 1/2 cup	**milk**
2 tablespoons	**butter** or **margarine**
1 teaspoon	**dried rosemary**
1 tablespoon	**garlic powder**
1 teaspoon	**salt**

Place potatoes in a soup pan and cover with water. Bring to a boil. Reduce to medium-low heat and cook 20–25 minutes. Drain water. Add milk, butter, rosemary, garlic powder, and salt. Mash with a potato masher or mix with an electric mixer. Serve immediately. Makes 5–6 servings.

CREAMY BAKED
MASHED POTATOES

4 cups	**mashed potatoes***
I package (8 ounces)	**cream cheese**
I can (10.5 ounces)	**cream of mushroom** or
	cream of chicken soup, condensed
¹/₄ cup	**chopped onion**
2	**eggs**
2 tablespoons	**flour**
I cup	**crushed cornflakes**

Preheat oven to 350 degrees. Mix potatoes, cream cheese, soup, onion, eggs, and flour together. Spread mixture into a greased 9 x 13-inch pan. Sprinkle cornflakes over top. Lightly press cornflakes into potato base. Bake 33–38 minutes, or until golden brown and warm in the center. Makes 8 servings.

* See page 10, Helpful Hints, for Mashed Potatoes recipe.

MASHED SWEET POTATOES

10 cups	**water**
1 teaspoon	**salt**
3	**large sweet potatoes,** peeled and cubed
1/4 cup	**butter** or **margarine**
1/2 cup	**orange juice**
1 1/2 tablespoons	**sugar**
1 1/2 cups	**mini marshmallows**

Preheat oven to 400 degrees.

Bring water and salt to a boil in a 4-quart pan. Add sweet potatoes and simmer over medium heat 17–22 minutes, or until potatoes are tender. Drain water and mash sweet potatoes in pan. Stir butter, orange juice, and sugar into hot potatoes. Spread into an 8 x 8-inch or 9 x 9-inch pan. Sprinkle marshmallows over top. Return to oven and bake 1–3 minutes, or until marshmallows are melted and a light golden brown. Makes 4–6 servings.

FRIES AND WEDGES

FAMILY FAVORITE FRENCH FRIES

5 **medium russet potatoes**
vegetable oil, for frying
salt, to taste

With or without skins, cut potatoes into ¼-inch-thick strips. Warm oil on high heat to 375 degrees in deep fry cooker or deep soup pan. Place a handful of potato strips in a metal strainer. Place strainer with potatoes in hot oil 3–4 minutes. Be sure strips are completely covered by oil (this prevents sticking). Cool on a cooling rack.* Repeat until all potato strips are done.

Once the entire batch is complete, allow oil to reach full heat again, then place a handful of cooked fries back in oil for 30 seconds to 2 minutes to create a crisp outside. Cool on cooling rack and add salt. Repeat until done.

Dip fries in ketchup, barbecue sauce, or ranch dressing. Makes 4–6 servings.

* Cooling racks that allow the oil to drip off work best. Place paper towels underneath to soak up excess oil.

CHILI CHEESE FRIES

16 ounces **frozen french fries***
1 can (15 ounces) **chili,** any variety
1 1/2 cups **grated cheddar cheese**

Prepare french fries according to package directions. Place hot fries on a large serving platter.

Warm chili in a saucepan over medium-low heat, then drizzle over fries. Top with grated cheddar cheese. Serve immediately. Makes 4–6 servings.

* Tater tots may be substituted.

BAKED OVEN FRIES

3 to 4 **medium russet potatoes**
$^1/_3$ cup **Miracle Whip**
1 teaspoon **garlic** or **onion salt**
$^1/_2$ teaspoon **pepper**

Preheat oven to 450 degrees.

With or without skins, cut potatoes into $^1/_2$-inch-thick strips. Shake cut potatoes and Miracle Whip together in a large zipper-lock plastic bag. Place potatoes on a baking sheet sprayed with vegetable oil. Sprinkle garlic salt and pepper over top. Bake 15–20 minutes. Remove from oven and flip potatoes. Bake an additional 15–20 minutes, or until fries reach desired crispness.

Dip fries in ketchup, honey mustard, or ranch dressing. Makes 3–5 servings.

PARMESAN POTATO SPEARS

3 to 4 **medium russet potatoes**
2 tablespoons **vegetable** or **olive oil**
2 tablespoons **grated Parmesan cheese**
1 teaspoon **salt**
$^1/_2$ teaspoon **paprika**
$^1/_8$ teaspoon **chili powder**

Preheat oven to 450 degrees.

With or without skins, cut potatoes into $^1/_2$-inch-thick strips. Place potatoes and vegetable oil in a large zipper-lock plastic bag. In a small bowl, combine Parmesan, salt, paprika, and chili powder. Sprinkle seasoning over potatoes in bag. Close bag and shake until all potatoes are evenly covered. Spread potatoes on a lightly greased baking sheet. Bake 15 minutes. Remove from oven and flip potatoes. Bake an additional 15–20 minutes, or until fries reach desired crispness. Makes 3–5 servings.

SWEET POTATO FRIES

2 **sweet potatoes**
canola or **vegetable oil,** for frying

Peel and cut potatoes into $1/4$-inch-thick strips. Warm oil on high heat to 375 degrees in deep fry cooker or deep soup pan. Cook a handful of sliced sweet potatoes at a time for $2^1/2$–4 minutes, or until golden brown. Be sure the strips are completely covered by oil (this prevents sticking).

Remove potatoes from oil with a slotted spatula or spoon and place on a cooling rack to cool.* Dab potatoes with paper towels to remove excess oil. Sprinkle with powdered sugar, cinnamon and sugar, or salt. Makes 2–4 servings.

* Cooling racks that allow the oil to drip off work best. Place paper towels underneath to soak up excess oil.

SKILLET FRIED RANCH POTATOES

2 tablespoons **olive oil**
4 cups **medium red potatoes,** diced
¼ cup **chopped onion**
I envelope **ranch dip mix**

Heat oil in a large frying pan over medium-high heat. Slowly add potatoes and onion to hot oil. Cover pan with a lid. Turn diced potatoes with a spatula every 2–3 minutes, or until golden brown. After 6 minutes of cooking, stir dry ranch dip mix into potatoes. Cook an additional 6–8 minutes, turning potatoes every 2–3 minutes. Makes 4–6 servings.

CHEESY BACON FRIES

16 ounces **frozen french fries***
3/4 cup **Cheez Whiz,** heated
1/8 cup **real bacon bits**
1/3 cup **sour cream**
2 tablespoons **sliced green onion,** optional

Prepare french fries according to package directions. Arrange hot, crisp fries on a serving platter. Pour hot cheese over fries. Sprinkle with bacon bits. Garnish with sour cream and green onion. Makes 4–6 servings.

* Tater tots may be substituted.

ITALIAN POTATO CHIPS

2 tablespoons **olive oil**
2 cups **red** or **russet potatoes,** thinly sliced
I teaspoon **Italian seasoning**
salt and pepper, to taste

Heat olive oil in a large frying pan over medium-high heat. Spread potatoes in hot oil. Cook, uncovered, for 5–6 minutes, or until golden brown. Flip potatoes. Sprinkle Italian seasoning evenly over top. Cook, uncovered, an additional 5–6 minutes. Place potatoes on a serving platter, add salt and pepper. Makes 2–3 servings.

CRISPY GARLIC MASHED POTATO BALLS

vegetable or **canola oil,** for frying
2 cups **warm mashed potatoes***
2 **eggs**
¹/₂ cup **flour**
¹/₂ cup **grated medium** or **sharp cheddar cheese**
1 teaspoon **garlic salt**
1 cup **seasoned bread crumbs**

Warm oil on high heat to 375 degrees in a soup pan. Mix together mashed potatoes, eggs, flour, cheese, and garlic salt until smooth. Place bread crumbs in a cereal bowl. Drop and roll balls of dough in bread crumbs.

Fry balls in hot oil 2–3 minutes, or until golden brown. Remove from oil with a slotted spatula or spoon and cool on a cooling rack.

Dip in ketchup or ranch dressing. Makes 4–6 servings.

* See page 10, Helpful Hints, for Mashed Potatoes recipe.

BAKED DIJON POTATO WEDGES

4	**medium red potatoes**
2 tablespoons	**Dijon mustard**
1 1/2 teaspoons	**paprika**
1 teaspoon	**ground cumin**
1/2 teaspoon	**garlic salt**

Preheat oven to 400 degrees. Spray a baking sheet with cooking spray.

Cut potatoes into wedges. Combine mustard, paprika, cumin, and garlic salt in a large bowl; mix well. Add potatoes to bowl; toss until completely coated. Spread wedges in a single layer on baking sheet. Bake 15 minutes, then turn potatoes. Bake an additional 10–15 minutes, or until potatoes are tender and golden brown.

Serve with honey mustard. Makes 2–4 servings.

BREAKFAST

COUNTRY HASH BROWNS

4 to 5	**medium russet potatoes**
1	**green** or **red bell pepper,** diced
¹/₂	**medium onion,** chopped
1 teaspoon	**paprika**
¹/₂ teaspoon	**salt**
¹/₄ teaspoon	**pepper**
3 tablespoons	**olive oil,** divided

Boil potatoes in their skins 20 minutes, or until about half cooked. Peel potatoes when cool enough to handle, then shred into a bowl. Stir in bell pepper, onion, paprika, salt, and pepper.

Heat 2 tablespoons oil in a large, nonstick frying pan. With a spatula, press potato mixture into hot oil.* Cook over low heat 15 minutes, or until bottom is golden brown. Loosen hash browns, then invert potatoes onto a plate. Add remaining 1 tablespoon oil to pan. Slide potatoes into pan white-side down. Cook 15 minutes, or until golden brown. Cut into wedges. Salt and pepper, to taste. Makes 4–6 servings.

* For crispier hash browns, cook half of the potato mixture at a time.

ONE-SKILLET BACON BREAKFAST

I to 2 tablespoons	**olive oil**
1 1/2 cups	**grated russet potato,** raw
I cup	**chopped onion**
4	**eggs,** beaten
3 slices	**bacon,** cooked and crumbled
	salt and pepper, to taste
4 to 6	**English muffins**

In a large frying pan, heat olive oil. Cook potatoes and onion in hot oil over medium-high heat, covered, 6–7 minutes. Stir and turn potatoes every 2–3 minutes, or until potatoes are tender and onions are transparent.

Pour beaten eggs and crumbled bacon over potato mixture. Sprinkle with salt and pepper. Reduce to medium-low heat. Cover and cook an additional 3 minutes. Flip egg and potato over, cover, and cook an additional 2–3 minutes, or until egg is thoroughly cooked. Serve on toasted English muffins. Makes 4–6 servings.

MORNING AFTER BAKED POTATO HASH BROWNS

2	**russet potatoes,** baked
2 tablespoons	**butter**
	seasoned salt, to taste*
	pepper, to taste

Grate leftover baked potatoes from last night's dinner into a frying pan with melted butter. Sprinkle seasonings over top. Cook over medium heat 10 minutes, turning occasionally. Makes 2 servings.

* Garlic salt or rosemary may be substituted.

SOUR CREAM POTATO PANCAKES

2	**medium russet potatoes,** grated and cooked
1	**small sweet onion,** chopped
1/2 cup	**dry pancake mix**
2 tablespoons	**sour cream**
3/4 teaspoon	**salt**
1/4 teaspoon	**pepper**

Mix all ingredients together in a bowl. Spoon batter into a hot, greased frying pan. Allow pancake bottom to brown. Flip and brown other side. Serve pancakes with sour cream, warm applesauce, or jam. Makes 4 servings.

BREAKFAST BURRITOS

4 **eggs**
I cup **potato,** shredded and boiled
$^1/_4$ cup **ground sausage** or **sliced sausage links,** cooked
$^1/_4$ cup **grated pepper jack** or **cheddar cheese**
2 to 3 **flour tortillas**
salsa
sour cream

Scramble eggs in a frying pan. Add potatoes to eggs and mix together lightly. Add sausage. Top with cheese and let it melt. Place mixture in tortillas. Serve with salsa and sour cream. Makes 2–3 servings.

HEARTY TURKEY BRUNCH SKILLET

¹/₂ cup	**chopped onion**
¹/₂ cup	**diced green bell pepper**
I can (14.5 ounces)	**diced new potatoes,** drained
I to 2 tablespoons	**vegetable** or **olive oil**
I cup	**diced cooked turkey breast**
6	**eggs,** beaten

In a large frying pan, saute onion, pepper, and potatoes in hot oil until tender. Stir in turkey. Pour eggs over top. Cover and simmer on low heat until eggs are done. Cut into wedges and serve. Makes 3–4 servings.

VARIATION: Make a scrambled egg skillet. Once eggs are added, stir until done.

BISCUITS WITH SAUSAGE GRAVY

2 cans (12 ounces each)	**Texas–style biscuits**
12 to 16 ounces	**Italian sausage,** browned and drained
2 cans (14.5 ounces each)	**diced new potatoes,** drained
2 cans (10.5 ounces each)	**cream of mushroom soup,** condensed
$1^3/_4$ cups	**water**
$1/_2$ teaspoon	**pepper**

Bake biscuits according to package directions and set aside. In a large frying pan, combine sausage and potatoes over medium-low heat. Cook 4–5 minutes, stirring every 60 seconds. Add soup, water, and pepper. Simmer on low heat an additional 5–7 minutes, or until thoroughly heated. Serve over biscuits. Makes 8–10 servings.

VARIATION: Make the sausage-and-potato gravy in a greased $2^1/_2$- to $3^1/_2$-quart slow cooker using $2^1/_2$ cups raw potatoes, peeled and diced. Do not used canned potatoes. Cover and cook on low heat 6–8 hours, or until potatoes are tender. Start slow cooker before you go to bed and wake up to an easy breakfast!

HAM-AND-CHEESE HASH BROWN OMELET

2 1/2 cups	**frozen shredded hash browns**
1/2 cup	**chopped onion**
	salt and pepper, to taste
4	**eggs,** beaten
1 cup	**cubed cooked ham***
4 slices	**Velveeta** or **cheddar cheese**
1 can (4 ounces)	**mushroom pieces,** drained

Place potatoes in a microwave-safe bowl. Microwave on high heat 4–6 minutes, or until potatoes are tender. (Potatoes will condense to approximately 2 cups upon being heated.) Add onion to hash browns, then spread mixture evenly over the bottom of a 10-inch nonstick frying pan.

In a separate bowl, add salt and pepper to eggs, then pour over potatoes, covering completely. Lay ham, cheese, and mushrooms over half the mixture. Cover and cook over medium-low heat 7–8 minutes, or until eggs are done and cheese is melted. With a spatula, fold omelet in half. Cut into wedges for individual servings. Makes 2–3 servings.

* Slices of ham lunch meat may be substituted.

SIMPLE BACON BREAKFAST PIE

          6 **medium eggs**
    $^1/_2$ cup **milk**
            salt and pepper, to taste
     3 cups **frozen shredded hash browns,** thawed
      I cup **grated Swiss cheese**
    $^1/_3$ cup **real bacon bits**

Preheat oven to 400 degrees.

In a 2-quart mixing bowl, whisk eggs, milk, salt, and pepper together.
Stir in hash browns, cheese, and bacon bits. Pour mixture into a greased
pie pan or 8 x 8-inch pan. Bake 30–35 minutes, or until center is set and
pie has turned golden brown. Cut into wedges. Makes 6–8 servings.

BREAKFAST CASSEROLE

$1/2$ pound	**sausage**
I teaspoon	**thyme**
3 cups	**frozen shredded hash browns,** thawed
6	**medium eggs**
$1/2$ cup	**milk**
I tablespoon	**dried minced onion**
	salt and pepper, to taste
I cup	**grated cheddar cheese**

Preheat oven to 400 degrees.

Brown and drain sausage in a frying pan. Add thyme and hash browns and set aside.

In a mixing bowl, whisk eggs, milk, onion, salt, and pepper together. Stir in sausage mixture and cheese. Pour into a greased 8 x 8-inch pan. Bake 30–35 minutes, or until center is set and pie has turned golden brown. Makes 4–6 servings.

SMOKED SAUSAGE AND EGG SKILLET

2 tablespoons	**vegetable** or **olive oil**
2 cups	**frozen southern-style cubed hash browns**
8 to 10	**little smoked sausages,** quartered
5	**eggs**
2 tablespoons	**milk**
1/4 teaspoon	**pepper**
1 teaspoon	**mustard,** optional
1/2 cup	**grated cheddar cheese**

Heat oil on medium-high heat in a large frying pan. Add hash browns and sausage to oil. Cook 5–7 minutes, turning potatoes 2 to 3 times until golden.

In a bowl, whisk eggs, milk, pepper, and mustard, if desired. Pour mixture over cooked potatoes. Cover and cook an additional 7–8 minutes over medium-low heat, or until eggs are completely cooked. Sprinkle cheese over top. Cut into wedges and serve. Makes 4–6 servings.

BREADS AND DESSERTS

GREAT GRANDMA'S SPUONUTS (IDAHO DONUTS)

2¹/₂ tablespoons	**active dry yeast**
¹/₂ cup	**warm water**
1 cup	**mashed potatoes,** unseasoned*
2 cups	**warm milk**
¹/₂ cup	**shortening**
1 cup	**sugar**
3	**eggs**
1¹/₂ teaspoons	**salt**
6 cups	**flour**
	vegetable oil, for frying
1 can (16 ounces)	**white frosting**
	chocolate syrup, maple flavor, to taste

Mix yeast, water, potatoes, and milk together. In a separate bowl, combine shortening, sugar, eggs, and salt. Stir mashed potato mixture into bowl with egg and shortening mixture. Stir in flour one cup at a time. Cover bowl with plastic wrap and allow dough to rise 45 minutes.

Roll out dough to ³/₄-inch thickness and cut with donut cutter. Fry dough in hot oil. Turn once, making sure donut is golden brown on both sides.

Divide frosting into three small bowls. Add chocolate syrup to one and maple flavor to another. Dip hot donuts into flavored frostings. For more variety, dip some into a mixture of cinnamon and sugar or powdered sugar. Makes 12–15 servings.

* See page 10, Helpful Hints, for Mashed Potatoes recipe. Do not use instant mashed potatoes for this recipe.

PEANUT BUTTER CHOCOLATE FUDGE

1 package (12 ounces)	**milk chocolate chips**
2 tablespoons	**milk**
1 cup	**chunky peanut butter**
1/2 cup	**warm mashed potatoes,** unseasoned*
1 teaspoon	**vanilla**
4 cups	**powdered sugar**
1/4 cup	**chopped peanuts**

In a nonstick saucepan, melt chocolate chips with milk over low heat, stirring constantly. Once completely melted, remove from heat and immediately stir in peanut butter, potatoes, and vanilla until smooth. Stir in powdered sugar, one cup at a time.

Press fudge into a lightly greased 8 x 8-inch or 9 x 9-inch pan. Sprinkle chopped nuts over top and lightly press into fudge. Cover and chill 2–3 hours. Cut and serve. Makes 12–16 servings.

* See page 10, Helpful Hints, for Mashed Potatoes recipe. Do not use instant mashed potatoes for this recipe.

FAMILY FAVORITE POTATO ROLLS

1 1/4 cups	**warm water**
1 teaspoon	**salt**
2 tablespoons	**vegetable** or **olive oil**
3 cups	**flour**
3/4 cup	**instant mashed potato flakes**
2 tablespoons	**nonfat dry milk**
1 tablespoon	**sugar**
2 1/4 teaspoons or	
1 envelope	**active dry yeast**
	butter

Add ingredients in the order listed above to bread machine pan.*
Select dough setting on your machine and press start. After 5–10
minutes, check dough. If needed, add 1 to 2 tablespoons water if
too dry or 1 to 2 tablespoons flour if too sticky.

Preheat oven to 350 degrees.

Form dough into 12 balls. Place into greased muffin pans. Allow
dough to rise 20–25 minutes, uncovered, in a draft-free area. Bake
18–22 minutes, or until golden brown. Brush tops with butter and
serve. Makes 12 servings.

* This recipe can also be made with a heavy-duty standing mixer.

POTATO BREAD

1 ¹/3 cups	**warm water**
1 ¹/2 tablespoons	**sugar***
2 teaspoons	**active dry yeast***
³/4 cup	**instant mashed potato flakes**
3 ¹/4 cups	**flour**
2 tablespoons	**nonfat dry milk**
2 tablespoons	**vegetable** or **olive oil**
1 teaspoon	**salt**

In a large bowl, mix water, sugar, yeast, and instant potato flakes together. Let stand 5 minutes. Mix in flour, dry milk, oil, and salt. Knead or mix in heavy-duty standing mixer 5–10 minutes.

Press dough into a greased 8¹/2 x 4¹/2-inch bread pan. Cover and let rise 40–45 minutes in a draft-free area.

Bake at 375 degrees 25 minutes. Cover with aluminum foil and bake an additional 12–18 minutes. Slice warm bread and serve with honey butter. Makes 6–8 servings.

* At altitudes above 3,500 feet, decrease sugar and yeast each by ¹/4 teaspoon.

SWEET POTATO ROLLS

2 1/4 teaspoons or
1 envelope **active dry yeast**
4 tablespoons **sugar,** divided
1/2 cup **warm water**
1 1/3 cups **canned sweet potatoes** or **yams,**
      drained and mashed
1/4 cup **butter** or **margarine,** softened
2 **eggs,** beaten
1 teaspoon **salt**
3 1/4 cups **flour**

Dissolve yeast and 1 tablespoon sugar in warm water. Let mixture sit 5 minutes.

Mash potatoes in a microwave-safe bowl and microwave 1 minute, or until warm. Add potatoes to yeast mixture. Mix in remaining sugar, butter, eggs, and salt until smooth. Stir in flour one cup at a time.

Knead by hand or by machine 1–3 minutes. Cover and allow dough to rise 50–60 minutes in a draft-free area. Punch down dough. Divide into 16 to 20 balls, adding small amounts of flour if needed to shape rolls. Place rolls in even rows in a greased 9 x 13-inch pan. Cover and allow rolls to rise 30–45 minutes, or until double in size.

Preheat oven to 350 degrees. Bake 16–20 minutes, or until golden brown. Makes 16–20 servings.

POTATO CHIP COOKIES

1	**white** or **yellow cake mix**
2	**eggs**
1/3 cup	**oil**
1 cup	**crushed plain potato chips**
3/4 cup	**milk chocolate chips**

Preheat oven to 350 degrees.

Mix together cake mix, eggs, and oil. Stir in crushed potato chips and chocolate chips. Drop teaspoon-sized dough balls onto a lightly greased baking sheet. Bake 8–10 minutes, or until light golden brown around edges. Makes 30–36 cookies.

COCONUT CHOCOLATE BARS

¹/₄ cup	**hot mashed potatoes,** unseasoned*
2 cups	**powdered sugar**
1 teaspoon	**corn syrup**
2 cups	**coconut**
1 teaspoon	**vanilla**
1 cup	**semi-sweet** or **milk chocolate chips**

Mix hot mashed potato with powdered sugar, corn syrup, coconut, and vanilla. Stir until well blended. Press into a lightly greased 8 x 8-inch pan or a pie pan.

Melt chocolate chips in a small saucepan over low heat, stirring constantly. Spread melted chocolate over coconut layer. Chill or freeze until chocolate hardens. Cut and serve. Makes 12–16 servings.

* See page 10, Helpful Hints, for Mashed Potatoes recipe. Do not use instant mashed potatoes for this recipe.

TRIPLE CHOCOLATE POTATO NUT CAKE

Cake:

1	**Betty Crocker Triple Chocolate Fudge cake mix**
3	**eggs**
1/3 cup	**butter** or **margarine,** melted
3/4 cup	**water**
1 cup	**mashed potatoes,** unseasoned*
1 cup	**semi-sweet chocolate chips**
1/2 cup	**chopped walnuts** or **pecans**

Glaze:

1 tablespoon	**butter**
3/4 cup	**semi-sweet chocolate chips**
2 tablespoons	**milk**
1/2 cup	**powdered sugar**

Preheat oven to 350 degrees.

With an electric mixer, mix cake mix, eggs, butter, water, and potatoes together 2–3 minutes. Stir in chocolate chips and nuts. Pour batter into a greased 9 x 13-inch pan. Bake 30–35 minutes, or until cake springs back when touched.

In a small saucepan, melt butter and chocolate chips into milk, stirring constantly. Remove from heat. Stir in powdered sugar. Drizzle glaze over warm cake. Makes 16–20 servings.

* See page 10, Helpful Hints, for Mashed Potatoes recipe. Do not use instant mashed potatoes for this recipe.

IVAN'S FAVORITE CARROT CAKE

1 **spice** or **carrot cake mix**
3 **eggs**
1 cup **mashed potatoes,** unseasoned*
$^1/_3$ cup **vegetable oil**
$^3/_4$ cup **water**
$^3/_4$ cup **grated carrots**
$^3/_4$ cup **Hershey's cinnamon chips**
  powdered sugar

Preheat oven to 350 degrees.

In a large bowl, mix cake mix, eggs, potatoes, oil, water, and carrots together. Stir in cinnamon chips. Pour into a greased 9 x 13-inch pan. Bake 30–35 minutes, or until cake springs back when touched.

Allow cake to cool. Sprinkle powdered sugar over top or frost with your favorite cream-cheese frosting. Makes 16 servings.

* See page 10, Helpful Hints, for Mashed Potatoes recipe. Do not use instant mashed potatoes for this recipe.

SWEET POTATO SPICE CRUNCH

I can (29 ounces) **sweet potatoes,** drained and mashed
2 **eggs,** beaten
I tablespoon **sugar**
I **spice cake mix**
$^1/_2$ cup **chopped pecans** or **almonds**
$^1/_2$ cup **butter** or **margarine,** melted

Preheat oven to 350 degrees.

Combine potatoes, eggs, and sugar. Press mixture into the bottom of a greased 9 x 13-inch pan. Sprinkle dry cake mix over mixture. Sprinkle nuts over top. Drizzle butter over dry cake mix. Bake 45–50 minutes, or until toothpick inserted in the center comes out clean. Cool and serve. Garnish with a dollop of whipped topping. Makes 16 servings.

CHOCOLATE CHIP
BANANA SPICE BREAD

1	**spice cake mix**
1 cup	**mashed potatoes,** unseasoned*
2	**eggs**
1/4 cup	**vegetable oil**
1/2 cup	**water**
2	**medium bananas,** mashed
1 cup	**mini chocolate chips**
	powdered sugar

Preheat oven to 350 degrees.

In a large bowl, mix cake mix, potatoes, eggs, oil, and water together until smooth. Stir in bananas and chocolate chips.

Divide batter between two greased, regular-size bread pans. Bake 35–40 minutes, or until toothpick comes out clean when inserted into center. Allow bread to cool to room temperature. Sprinkle powdered sugar over loaves, slice, and serve. Makes 12–16 servings.

* See page 10, Helpful Hints, for Mashed Potatoes recipe. Do not use instant mashed potatoes for this recipe.

SWEET POTATO CHEESECAKE

2 packages (8 ounces each) **cream cheese,** softened
¾ cup **canned sweet potatoes,** drained and mashed
½ cup **sugar**
1 teaspoon **pumpkin pie spice**
½ teaspoon **vanilla**
2 **eggs**
1 (6-ounce) **pre-made graham cracker pie crust**

Preheat oven to 350 degrees.

In a medium bowl, mix cream cheese, potatoes, sugar, spice, and vanilla until smooth. Mix in eggs one at a time until thoroughly blended. Spread into crust. Bake 40–45 minutes, or until center is set. Allow to cool.

Use plastic liner from pie crust to cover cooled cheesecake. Refrigerate 3–4 hours or overnight. Serve with a dollop of whipped topping or with butterscotch or caramel ice cream topping drizzled over individual servings. Makes 6–8 servings.

NOTES

NOTES

NOTES

ABOUT THE AUTHOR

Stephanie Ashcraft was raised near Kirklin, Indiana. She received a bachelor's degree in family science and a teaching certificate from Brigham Young University. Stephanie loves teaching and spending time with friends and family. Since 1998, she has taught cooking classes throughout the state of Utah. She and her husband, Ivan, reside in Rexburg, Idaho, with their children. Being a mom is her full-time job.